1020407

D0792315

[DISCARDED

WHAT COLOR IS THAT DINOSAUR?

Questions, Answers, and Mysteries

BY LOWELL DINGUS
Illustrations by
STEPHEN C. QUINN

The Millbrook Press
Brookfield, Connecticut

Library of Congress Cataloging-in-Publication Data
Dingus, Lowell.
What color is that dinosaur? : questions, answers, and mysteries /
by Lowell Dingus; illustrations by Stephen C. Quinn.
p. cm.
Includes bibliographical references and index.
Summary: Answers questions about dinosaurs and explains how
today's scientists are trying to learn more about prehistory's most
fascinating creatures.
ISBN 1-56294-365-0 (lib. bdg.) ISBN 1-56294-728-1 (pbk.)
1. Dinosaurs—Juvenile literature. [1. Dinosaurs.] I. Quinn,
Stephen C., 1951– ill. II. Title. III. Series.
QE862.D5D493 1994
567.9′1—dc20   93-10664 CIP AC

Published by The Millbrook Press
2 Old New Milford Road
Brookfield, Connecticut 06804

Copyright © 1994 by Lowell Dingus
All rights reserved
Printed in the United States of America
1   3   5   4   2

CONTENTS

WHAT COLOR IS THAT DINOSAUR?

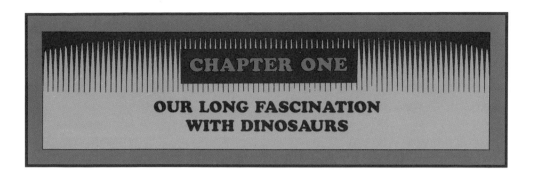

CHAPTER ONE

OUR LONG FASCINATION WITH DINOSAURS

The first dinosaur bones were discovered about two hundred years ago in England. Ever since that time, dinosaurs have had a special appeal for people of all ages. Men, women, and children flocked to the first exhibit of dinosaurs, which opened at England's Crystal Palace in 1853. To celebrate the opening, the scientist who coined the term "dinosaur," Sir Richard Owen, threw a dinner party for twenty guests inside a model of the dinosaur *Iguanodon*. Even though the guests were rather cramped and the model was not very accurate, the dinner was a great success. Today, dinosaurs are more popular than ever.

Dinosaurs evolved into a dazzling variety of sizes and shapes. Brachiosaurus, *a giant plant-eating sauropod, stood almost 50 feet (15 meters) tall, while* Compsognathus, *a small carnivorous theropod, stood only 12 inches (30 centimeters) tall. Both these dinosaurs lived about 150 million years ago.*

7

The fearsome carnivore Tyrannosaurus stalks a herd of the plant-eating, horned dinosaur Torosaurus from the edge of a forest about 65 million years ago.

Why have dinosaurs captured our interest for such a long time? Well, words like "mysterious," "ancient," "strange," "fearsome," and "huge" all apply, at least in some cases. Even though dinosaurs really lived, they seem like something out of our imagination or a science-fiction movie. Because they're so fascinating and mysterious, we want to know everything about them.

But what do we really know about dinosaurs, and how do we know it? What might we be able to guess about them by looking at animals living today? And finally, what don't we know about dinosaurs?

In the pages that follow, we'll explore what paleontologists—the scientists who study dinosaurs—have learned in the two centuries since dinosaurs were first discovered. We'll also look into some of the mysteries that have yet to be solved.

CHAPTER TWO

HOW DO WE KNOW THAT
DINOSAURS REALLY LIVED?

Exploring the past takes a special kind of detective work on the part of paleontologists. To learn more about animals that have lived in the past, paleontologists must look for clues preserved in ancient rocks. These clues are called fossils. Fossils are the remains of ancient life, such as shells of animals that once lived in the ocean or the leaves and stems of plants that lived on land. We know that dinosaurs lived because we find their bones, teeth, and footprints preserved as fossils.

Looking for fossils is the best part about being a paleontologist. It's the grandest possible treasure hunt. But fossils can be hard to find, because only a few of the animals and plants that have lived in the past have been preserved as fossils. That's because it takes a lot of very unusual conditions to create a fossil.

The process of fossilization began after a dinosaur died. Usually, the soft parts of the carcass, such as flesh and hair, decayed quickly. Only the hard parts, such as bones and teeth, remained lying on the surface of the ground. Occasionally, the skeleton was quickly covered by layers of sand and mud carried by ancient

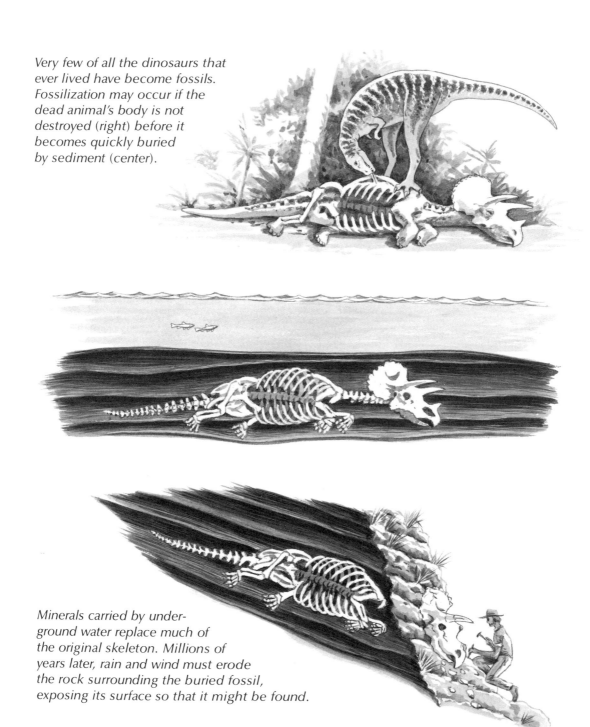

Very few of all the dinosaurs that ever lived have become fossils. Fossilization may occur if the dead animal's body is not destroyed (right) before it becomes quickly buried by sediment (center).

Minerals carried by underground water replace much of the original skeleton. Millions of years later, rain and wind must erode the rock surrounding the buried fossil, exposing its surface so that it might be found.

rivers or laid down in the bottom of ancient lakes. Over a very long time, minerals in the water that seeped down through the sand and mud replaced much of the original bone material. When that happened, the minerals formed a rock that had the same shape as the bone, and this rock, called a fossil, could last for millions of years.

Eventually, the other rocks that surrounded the buried fossil bone were gradually removed by wind or by water in modern streams. And if you are lucky, you may find the fossilized bone or tooth of the long-dead dinosaur lying on the surface of the ground.

Usually, most of the fossil bone or skeleton is still embedded in the rock, and it takes special skill to remove the fossil without damage. There are often many breaks in the stone that makes up the fossil. To get the fossil safely back home to the museum or university, the paleontologist builds a plaster cast around it, in the same way a doctor puts a plaster cast around a broken arm or leg.

Discovering and collecting fossil bones and teeth is just the first step in the dinosaur detective story. By studying the shapes of the fossil bones and comparing them to the bones of living animals, scientists may learn that the fossil bones do not belong to any species of animal living now. Scientists work to figure out how the fossil bones fit together in order to understand what the animal might have looked like and who its closest relatives were. They study the rocks in which the fossils are found to discover how long ago the dinosaur lived and what the environment was like. All in all, dinosaurs make up only one chapter in a much longer story that involves many animals and events both before and since the Age of Dinosaurs.

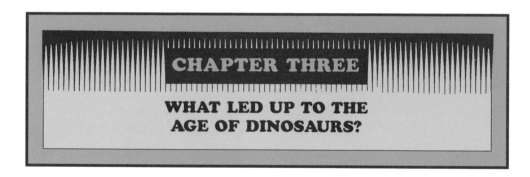

CHAPTER THREE

WHAT LED UP TO THE AGE OF DINOSAURS?

Everyone has a family history. Before you came along, there were your parents and grandparents, and before them, your great-grandparents. Some families can trace their ancestors back for hundreds of years. When you stretch hundreds of years into thousands and millions of years, you begin to talk about the ancestry of all humans. As scientists try to trace the history of life back further and further, it becomes harder and harder to tell exactly who descended from whom, but we can still tell close relatives from more distant relatives. By looking for fossils of very ancient animals, we can explore the early family history of dinosaurs.

Scientists have discovered a number of events that led up to the origin of dinosaurs. The development of dinosaurs from earlier ancestors as conditions on Earth changed over very long periods of time is a spectacular example of the process of evolution.

The long sequence of evolutionary events that resulted in the rise of dinosaurs began at least 3.5 billion years ago. This was the time of the earliest-known forms of life on Earth. Some of these one-celled life-forms were preserved as fossils in ancient rocks. Amazingly, they look much like some kinds of blue-green algae still living in oceans and lakes today. To the best of our knowledge, one of these earliest microscopic life-forms was the ancestor of all living things, including dinosaurs and you.

Much later, about 500 million years ago, the first fishlike animals with backbones appeared in the oceans. These earliest animals with backbones were small and covered with bone that may have served to protect them from predators hunting for food. All animals with a backbone belong to a group called vertebrates, named for the individual bones, or vertebrae, that make up the backbone. Because you have a backbone, you're a member of this group. So were dinosaurs.

It wasn't until about 350 million years ago that the first four-legged animals with well-developed arms, legs, fingers, and toes walked out of watery environments to begin living part of their life on land. All animals with four limbs are called tetrapods, which means "four-footed." These earliest-known land dwellers appear to be distantly related to living frogs and salamanders, although some grew to a length of several feet! The tetrapod group also includes dinosaurs and humans, since we all have well-developed arms and legs.

About 50 million years later, the branch of the evolutionary tree leading toward dinosaurs split from the branch leading toward mammals, including you. This important event was marked by the development of the first watertight egg. This kind of egg, so familiar in the supermarket, is laid not only by hens and other birds, but also by turtles, lizards, crocodiles, and even primitive mammals such as the platypus. All these animals are called amniotes, a name that refers to the watertight membrane called the amnion that surrounds the developing baby inside the egg. Unlike eggs laid in the water by fish and frogs, this new kind of egg with its protective shell could be laid on land because it would not dry out, thus killing the baby developing inside.

Still, another 75 million years would pass before the earliest dinosaurs that we know about appeared on the Earth.

The earliest-known single-celled life-forms lived in the oceans several billion years ago. About 600 million years ago, animals with more than one cell, such as trilobites, jellyfish, and sea scorpions became common (lower left). Vertebrates arose about 500 million years ago, but they did not move onto land until about 350 million years ago. Another 125 million years passed before the first-known dinosaur arose (upper right).

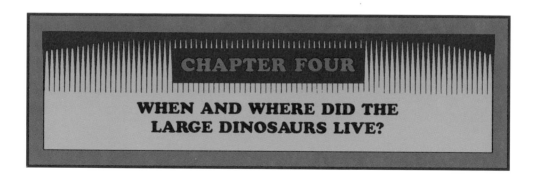

CHAPTER FOUR

WHEN AND WHERE DID THE LARGE DINOSAURS LIVE?

The earliest dinosaurs that we know about, such as *Herrerasaurus*, lived about 228 million years ago, long before there were any humans on the Earth. We know how long ago the earliest-known dinosaurs lived because we have special scientific instruments that can measure the age of the rocks in which dinosaur fossils have been found. The last large dinosaur died out about 65 million years ago.

The stretch of time from about 228 to 65 million years ago, often called the Age of Dinosaurs, is a very long period. For example, humans have been living on the Earth for only 4 million years. Think about how long it will be until you are 50 years old, and then try to imagine 200 million years! We'll talk more in chapters 7 and 8 about when different kinds of dinosaurs lived.

When the first dinosaurs were alive, the Earth had just one large landmass, or continent, called Pangaea, surrounded by a gigantic ocean. Since that time, sections of this ancient landmass have been slowly drifting apart, forming today's continents.

Fossils of dinosaurs have been found on every continent of today's world—from the icy landscapes of the Arctic and Antarc-

One of the earliest and most primitive
dinosaurs known was the carnivore
Herrerasaurus. It was about 10 feet
(3 meters) long and stood about
5 feet (1.5 meters) tall.

135 MILLION YEARS AGO

LAURASIA

GONDWANA

200 MILLION YEARS AGO

PANGAEA

North America Europe Asia

South America Africa India

Antarctica Australia

65 MILLION YEARS AGO

North America Europe Asia

Africa India

South America

Australia

Antarctica

TODAY

tic to the steamy jungles of central Africa to the dry, blistering hot deserts of central Asia. Some of the richest "treasure chests" of dinosaur fossils have been found in North America, especially in Montana, Wyoming, Colorado, Utah, New Mexico, Arizona, South Dakota, and Alberta, Canada. During the last part of the Age of Dinosaurs, a shallow sea extended through the middle of the continent from the Gulf of Mexico up to the Arctic Ocean. Thousands and thousands of dinosaurs, including *Apatosaurus* (formerly known as *Brontosaurus*), *Allosaurus*, *Stegosaurus*, *Triceratops*, and *Tyrannosaurus*, lived along the shores of that seaway at various times during the Age of Dinosaurs.

Actually, dinosaurs still live all over the world. The idea may sound a bit ridiculous, but we'll get to that story later.

CHAPTER FIVE

WHAT MAKES A DINOSAUR DIFFERENT FROM OTHER ANIMALS?

Many people think that a dinosaur is any kind of large animal that became extinct, or died out, long ago. But that is not correct.

Scientists sort animals into family groups by looking for features that different animals share in their body structure. Dinosaurs have a hole in the bones that form the roof, or top, of the mouth. This hole is found only in turtles, lizards, snakes, crocodiles, birds, and their relatives. We are not sure what purpose this hole serves, but the fact that dinosaurs have it means that they belong to this large group of animals. Some scientists call the members of this family reptiles, but others prefer to call them sauropsids.

Dinosaurs do not belong to the group that includes saber-toothed cats, mastodons, mammoths, and giant ground sloths. These extinct animals had skulls that were constructed more like ours. Animals in this group have a special hole in the skull behind the eye socket. Muscles that close the jaws attach to the bone surrounding this hole. On your skull, this hole lies between your cheekbone and your temple. When you bite down hard, you can

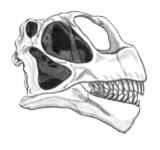

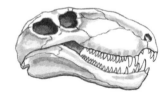

CAMARASAURUS   HUMAN   DIMETRODON

The earliest reptiles, or sauropsids, had no hole in the skull behind each eye socket. Dinosaurs, however, have two holes in that position. All mammals and their extinct relatives have only one hole in the skull behind each eye socket.

feel the jaw muscles that attach to the bone around the hole contract! This means that you also belong to this group, called synapsids, that includes mammals and their early relatives. Unlike dinosaurs, mammals have hair, as you do, and feed their newborn babies with milk, just as your mother fed you when you were a baby.

Dinosaurs are reptiles, or sauropsids, with legs that go straight down from their body to the ground. They're built differently from other reptiles, including turtles, lizards, and crocodiles, which have legs that stick out from the sides of their body.

Some extinct reptiles that are often called dinosaurs don't have legs like these. For instance, ichthyosaurs, plesiosaurs, mosasaurs, and pterosaurs are all on the list of reptiles that do not qualify as dinosaurs. As you can see, their legs don't go straight down from the body. Ichthyosaurs, plesiosaurs, and mosasaurs did not walk or run on land; instead, they swam in the ocean. We know that because their arms and legs formed flippers somewhat similar to a dolphin's. In addition, fossil skeletons of ichthyosaurs, plesiosaurs, and mosasaurs are always found in rocks that were formed at the bottom of ancient oceans.

The legs of most reptiles, or sauropsids, extend out to the side of the body, as shown by the Nile crocodile (bottom). Dinosaurs are unique among reptiles in having legs that extend straight down to the ground from the hips, as shown by Camarasaurus (top).

Mosasaurs (top), plesiosaurs (center), and ichthyosaurs (bottom) are three groups of marine reptiles, or sauropsids, that lived at the same time as the large dinosaurs. The structure of their limbs shows that they were not dinosaurs.

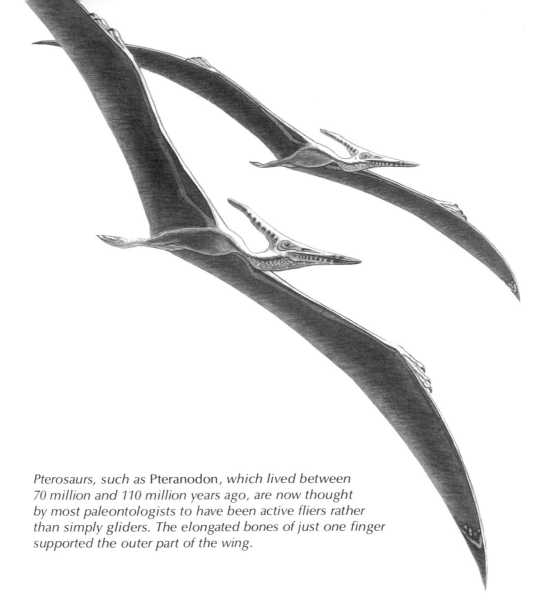

Pterosaurs, such as Pteranodon, *which lived between 70 million and 110 million years ago, are now thought by most paleontologists to have been active fliers rather than simply gliders. The elongated bones of just one finger supported the outer part of the wing.*

Pterosaurs are closely related to dinosaurs, but their thigh bones did not quite come straight down from their hips. Pterosaurs also had wings and flew through the air. However, their wings were built very differently from a bird's or a bat's. Most of the length of a bird's wing is formed by the large arm bone attached to the shoulder and by the bones between the elbow and the wrist. In pterosaurs, most of the length of the wing is formed by the bones of just one finger—the same finger that we call our ring finger!

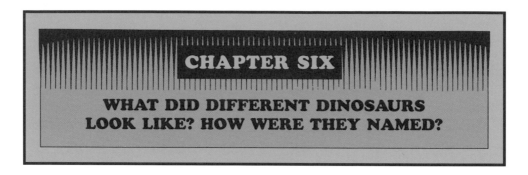

CHAPTER SIX

WHAT DID DIFFERENT DINOSAURS LOOK LIKE? HOW WERE THEY NAMED?

Dinosaurs that lived millions of years ago came in all sizes. Some were as small as a rooster, while others may have been more than 100 feet (30 meters) long and weighed more than 75 tons. We know about this great range in size from the sizes of dinosaur bones that have been preserved as fossils.

Usually only part of an individual dinosaur skeleton is found. This might happen for several reasons. After the dinosaur died, the river currents carrying the sand and mud that buried the skeleton could have been strong enough to scatter the bones into different places along the riverbed. Or perhaps another dinosaur tore apart the carcass and carried it off to a different place to eat it. It is hard to be certain why we usually find only parts of skeletons. Rarely, though, all the bones of an individual dinosaur are found. By studying how the bones fit together, paleontologists can figure out how big the whole animal was.

Besides coming in many different sizes, extinct dinosaurs also came in many shapes. Again, we know about these differences from the shape of the bones in the fossil skeletons, which give us a rough idea of the shape of that particular kind of dinosaur. However, the muscles that attached to the skeleton are not preserved as fossils. So we can only guess what the living animals might have looked like by putting the same muscles on skeletons of extinct dinosaurs that we find in the bodies of their closest living relatives, birds and crocodiles.

The variety of shapes and sizes seen in different kinds of dinosaurs is matched by the names we have given them. Each dinosaur has two scientific names, such as *Tyrannosaurus rex*. (Scientists give similar names to other living things. The two-part scientific name for humans is *Homo sapiens*.) The first name is always capitalized, and both names are spelled with slanted, or italic, letters. The second name is not capitalized.

Sometimes the name of a dinosaur is meant to describe how the dinosaur behaved or looked. For example, *Tyrannosaurus* means "tyrant lizard." The dinosaur might also be named for the place where its fossils were first found. *Albertosaurus* was a close relative of *Tyrannosaurus* that was first found in Alberta, Canada, for example. Other dinosaurs are named in honor of a person, such as a famous fossil collector or paleontologist. *Protoceratops andrewsi*, for example, was named after the famous American paleontologist Roy Chapman Andrews, who found many important fossils in the Gobi Desert of Mongolia.

All these dinosaurs, no matter what their size, shape, or name, belong to one of two large dinosaur families: the saurischians or the ornithischians. The difference between the two families is found in the bones of their skeletons.

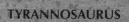

TYRANNOSAURUS

This family tree of saurischian dinosaurs shows which were most closely related and when they lived. The lineage containing Archaeopteryx continues right up to the present in the form of modern birds.

VELOCIRAPTOR

CRETACEOUS

ARCHAEOPTERYX

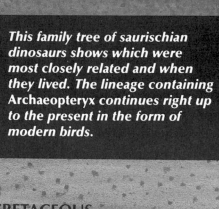

BAROSAURUS

BRACHIOSAURUS

JURASSIC

PLATEOSAURUS

HERRERASAURUS

TRIASSIC

CHAPTER SEVEN

WHICH DINOSAURS BELONGED TO THE SAURISCHIAN FAMILY?

Let's look first at the family called saurischians, a name that means "lizard-hipped." It's true that saurischians have hipbones constructed like those of lizards. However, the unique features of saurischians are their relatively long necks and their hands, or front feet, which have a thumb that is set off from the rest of the fingers. This arrangement is somewhat similar to the way your hand is constructed. Like you, many saurischians may have been able to grasp pieces of food or other objects with their hands.

The family of saurischians includes the giant herbivorous, or plant-eating, dinosaurs (sauropods) and their early relatives, as well as the carnivorous, or meat-eating, dinosaurs (theropods). The sauropod group contains the largest land animals ever known to have lived. Even the earliest members of this group, such as *Plateosaurus*, which lived in Europe around 200 million years ago, had a fairly long neck and tail attached to a stout body—features that would become even more highly developed in the peak time of giant dinosaurs.

That time occurred about 150 million years ago, when numerous sauropods inhabited North America, South America,

29

Asia, and Africa. They included *Apatosaurus*, *Diplodocus*, *Camarasaurus*, *Brachiosaurus*, *Barosaurus*, and *Mamenchisaurus*. All had an extremely long neck and an enormous body. Others, such as the *Seismosaurus*, *Ultrasaurus*, and *Supersaurus*, may have been as much as 100 feet (30 meters) long and weighed 70 to 80 tons, but we have to find more complete skeletons of them to be sure.

The other group of saurischians, the meat-eating theropods, contains the most fearsome and famous dinosaur of all, *Tyrannosaurus rex*. Unlike the thickly walled bones of the giant sauropods, the bones of these meat eaters had relatively thin walls. Also, their hind feet had three fully developed toes that

point forward, with the middle toe the longest. One large group of animals living today has bones and feet built this way.

Not all the meat eaters were huge like *T. rex*, which lived near the end of the Age of Dinosaurs about 65 million years ago, or like *Allosaurus*, which lived about 150 million years ago and was 25 feet (7.6 meters) or more in length. One of the earliest ones we know about, *Coelophysis*, lived in North America just over 200 million years ago. It grew to be only about 5 feet (1.5 meters) long from its nose to the end of its tail and stood only about 4 feet (1.2 meters) tall. *Compsognathus*, which lived in Europe at about the same time that *Allosaurus* was terrorizing North America, was only the size of a crow!

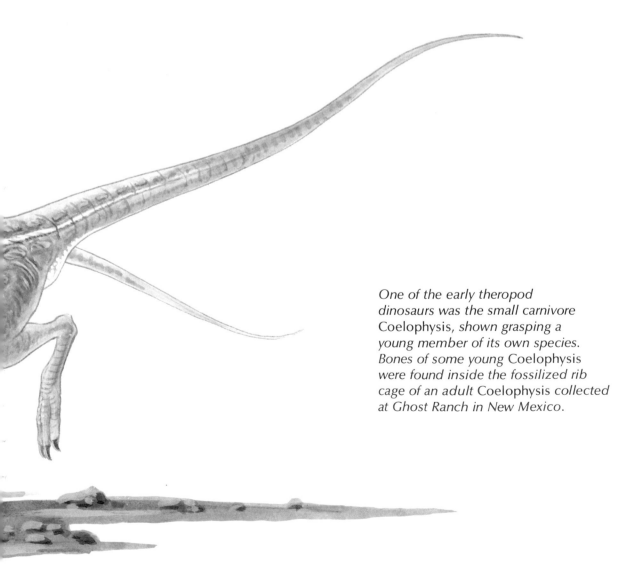

One of the early theropod dinosaurs was the small carnivore Coelophysis, *shown grasping a young member of its own species. Bones of some young* Coelophysis *were found inside the fossilized rib cage of an adult* Coelophysis *collected at Ghost Ranch in New Mexico.*

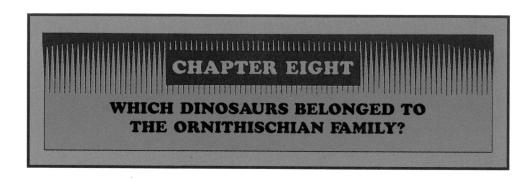

CHAPTER EIGHT

WHICH DINOSAURS BELONGED TO THE ORNITHISCHIAN FAMILY?

The term ornithischian means "bird-hipped." However, the name is misleading, because these dinosaurs are not very closely related to birds. The ornithischians all have a special bone in the hip, called the pubis, that points toward the rear of the animal. This feature is seen even in the earliest-known ornithischian, *Lesothosaurus*, which lived in Africa about 200 million years ago. It's hard to be sure what advantage, if any, this feature might have given these animals because no ornithischians are alive for us to observe today. Perhaps it provided added support for the stomach and intestines. Within the group called ornithischians there are five smaller groups—including some with tongue-twisting names: stegosaurs, ankylosaurs, hadrosaurs (or duckbills) and their early relatives, pachycephalosaurs, and ceratopsians.

Stegosaurs and ankylosaurs are unique in having extensive shields, plates, or spikes of bony armor that cover much of their body. The first sign of this armor covering was present in *Scutellosaurus*, which lived in North America almost 200 million years ago. This dinosaur was the earliest close relative of ankylosaurs and stegosaurs.

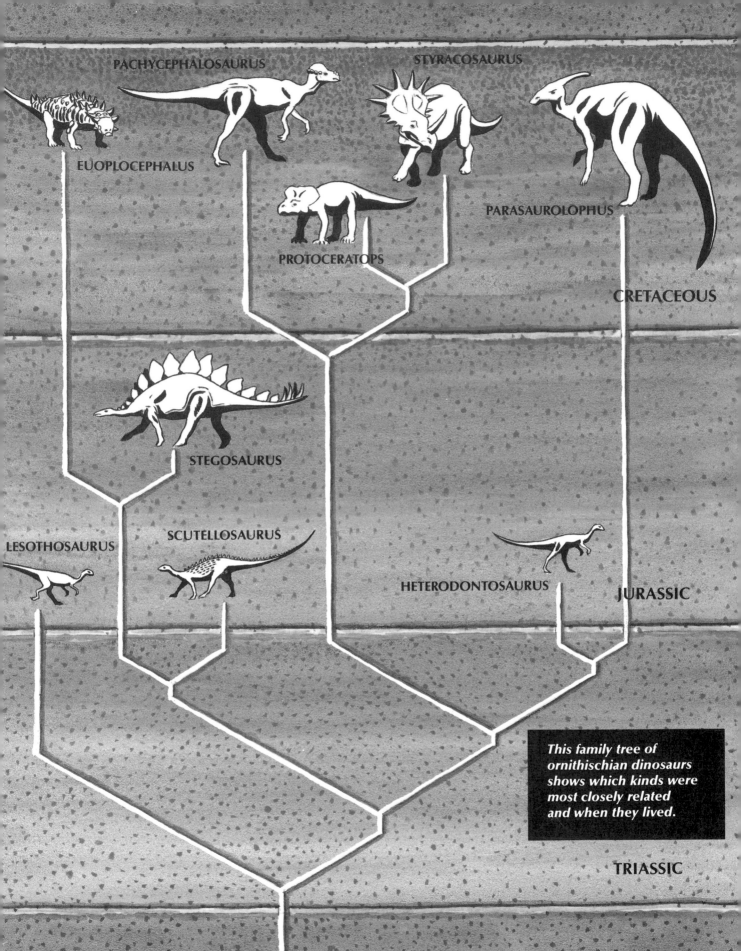

PACHYCEPHALOSAURUS

STYRACOSAURUS

EUOPLOCEPHALUS

PROTOCERATOPS

PARASAUROLOPHUS

CRETACEOUS

STEGOSAURUS

SCUTELLOSAURUS

LESOTHOSAURUS

HETERODONTOSAURUS

JURASSIC

This family tree of ornithischian dinosaurs shows which kinds were most closely related and when they lived.

TRIASSIC

A stegosaur's armor lies along the middle of the body above the backbone. It consists of large bony plates, which usually extend from the neck to back near the hips, and bony spikes, which extend from around the hips to near the back of the tail. Most stegosaurs, including *Stegosaurus* itself, lived about 150 million years ago. Their fossils have been found mostly in North America, Europe, and Asia.

Most paleontologists suspect that a stegosaur used its spikes for defense by swinging its tail at an attacking predator. But they still argue over exactly what the plates were used for. Did the plates simply provide protection to keep predators from biting the stegosaur on the neck or back? Or might they have helped the animal to warm up, by absorbing heat from sunlight, or cool down when the animal moved into the shade? Since stegosaurs are all extinct, we cannot watch to see how they defended themselves or measure their body temperature. And how they used their plates remains a mystery.

The other group of armored dinosaurs, ankylosaurs, had a more complete coat of bony armor. Most ankylosaurs lived during the last part of the Age of Dinosaurs, between 130 million and 65 million years ago. The later ankylosaurs are noteworthy for the clubs of bone that grew at the end of their tails. The ankylosaur probably used the club to help defend itself against predators.

Duckbills and their relatives make up another group of ornithischians. All had a specially placed joint between the upper and lower jaw, which may have aided in grinding the tough plant parts that they ate. The earliest-known members of the group, such as *Heterodontosaurus*, from Africa, lived almost 200 million years ago.

A later and better known member of this group is the 120-million-year-old *Iguanodon*, famous for the spike of bone on the end of its thumb. When fossil collectors first found examples of this spike, it was thought to have been attached to the end of the animal's nose!

34

Some of the heavily armored ankylosaurs sported tail clubs that may have served as formidable defensive weapons. An example is Euoplocephalus, *which lived about 70 million years ago, at the same time as* Albertosaurus.

But the duckbills, or hadrosaurs, are the most famous members of the group. They all had tremendously enlarged bones around the nasal opening, or nostril. In some forms, such as *Parasaurolophus* and *Corythosaurus*, these bones grew into elaborate crests on top of the head. The duckbills lived relatively late in the Age of Dinosaurs, with most forms inhabiting Asia and North America between 90 and 65 million years ago.

Many paleontologists have tried to figure out how duckbills used their crest. One early idea was that it could be filled with air to help the duckbill stay submerged longer when the animal was in the water. But not enough air could be stored in the crest to allow the animal to stay underwater for very long. More recently, paleontologists have suggested that the crest may have served as a trumpet through which the animal called to other duckbills. Or it may have been a visual signal to attract mates or scare off rivals, like the feathery display of the peacock. Perhaps one or both of these ideas are correct. However, because no duckbills are alive for us to observe, we just cannot be sure.

The horned dinosaurs, ceratopsians, and the bone-headed dinosaurs, pachycephalosaurs, are unique in having a shelf of bone that grows around the back of the skull. In the ceratopsians, the shelf extended to the rear, forming a shield that covered the neck. However, the shelf in pachycephalosaurs fused with other bones on top of the skull to form a thick dome or helmet of bone. These two groups were also latecomers in the Age of Dinosaurs.

Vocal calls may have played important roles between dinosaurs involved in mating, herding, or rearing young, as shown by these two Parasaurolophus. *Unfortunately, fossils don't provide many clues about how or why dinosaurs might have called to one another.*

36

Most forms inhabited North America and Asia between 100 million and 65 million years ago.

As the name implies, all but the earliest horned dinosaurs have an array of bony horns on their skull. One of the earlier members of the group, *Protoceratops*, played an important role in the history of our knowledge about dinosaurs. In 1923 a group of collectors from the American Museum of Natural History in New York, led by Roy Chapman Andrews, discovered the first known dinosaur eggs in nests of *Protoceratops* that lived in Mongolia, in the middle of Asia.

Later ceratopsians, such as *Triceratops*, *Styracosaurus*, *Torosaurus*, and *Pentaceratops*, lived on the coastal plain bordering the shallow sea that extended from the Gulf of Mexico up to the Arctic Ocean during the last 15 million years of the Age of Dinosaurs.

What did ceratopsians use the horns and shields for? At first paleontologists thought that they were defensive weapons, like the shields and swords of medieval knights. But recently, artists have suggested that the shields may have been covered with brightly colored skin to attract mates or scare off rivals. Again, the correct answer remains a mystery since all the horned dinosaurs are extinct, so we cannot go out and watch them.

Fossils of bone-headed dinosaurs, pachycephalosaurs, are found mostly in Asia and North America. Although they are easily distinguished from other dinosaurs because of the helmet of bone on top of the skull, most kinds of pachycephalosaurs are not well known from fossils. They vary in size from animals less than 5 feet (1.5 meters) long to the giant *Pachycephalosaurus* itself, which may have been more than 25 feet (7.6 meters) long.

The thick bony helmet that formed the top of a Pachycephalosaurus *skull may have been used for butting other pachycephalosaurs or for other purposes.*

The bony helmet, sometimes as much as 6 inches (15 centimeters) thick, has caused many paleontologists to wonder about its purpose. Most guesses have proposed that pachycephalosaurs butted heads, the way modern mountain sheep do. There is some evidence to support this idea. The head fits onto the backbone in a way that would make head-butting possible, and the backbones themselves fit together very snugly, which could have helped absorb the shock of ramming and prevented the backbones from twisting and injuring the animal. Head-butting may have been directed at attacking predators or used in competition for mates.

Although these ideas are intriguing, it is not possible to be certain if pachycephalosaurs actually butted heads. Like other large, ancient dinosaurs, all the pachycephalosaurs are extinct, so we cannot see how they behaved.

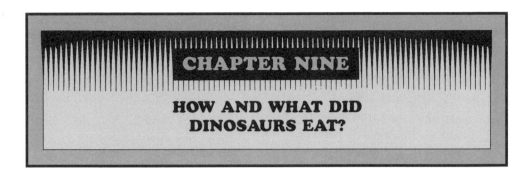

CHAPTER NINE

HOW AND WHAT DID DINOSAURS EAT?

Dozens of kinds of dinosaurs dominated the Earth for many millions of years. As might be expected, this very large group not only varied in size and shape but also had a variety of habits, including differences in the food they ate. Of course, we can't watch these vanished dinosaurs, and so we cannot be certain exactly what any particular kind of dinosaur included in its diet. But in many cases, we can make a general guess by looking at the shape of a dinosaur's tooth and comparing it to the teeth of living animals.

When we find a living animal with a tooth shaped like that of a dinosaur, we can guess that the dinosaur ate a similar kind of food, because certain kinds of food are best broken up into bits before swallowing by certain kinds of teeth. A lion, for example, needs teeth with sharp points and edges to tear up meat. A horse needs teeth with a flat top for grinding up the grass it eats. You have some of both these kinds of teeth so that you can chew both meat and vegetables. Studying the shape of teeth in different dinosaurs suggests that some probably ate meat, and others probably ate plants.

41

Dinosaurs such as *Tyrannosaurus*, *Allosaurus*, and *Deinonychus* all had teeth with sharp points and jagged edges. If you look closely at the edge of a tooth from one of these dinosaurs, you'll see that it looks a lot like the cutting blade on a steak knife. Living sharks have pointed teeth with jagged cutting edges that are generally similar to those of *Tyrannosaurus* and *Allosaurus*. For these reasons, almost all paleontologists think that *Allosaurus*, *Tyrannosaurus*, *Deinonychus*, and their close relatives ate meat.

In contrast to *Tyrannosaurus* and *Deinonychus*, other dinosaurs, such as *Triceratops* and the duckbill *Anatotitan*, had teeth with smooth flat surfaces on top rather than sharp points with jagged edges. Modern cattle and horses also have teeth with flat tops for grinding up grasses that serve as their main source of food. After comparing the teeth, most paleontologists believe that *Triceratops* and *Anatotitan* also ate plants. Some rather certain evidence about the diet of duckbills was found when a paleontologist studied the stomach contents of one very well-preserved fossil "mummy." In the stomach area, seeds, twigs, and needles like those from living pine trees were found. Unfortunately, fossils of most kinds of dinosaurs are not so well preserved, so that more uncertainty exists about their exact diet.

Interestingly, we know that when the teeth of *Anatotitan* and *Triceratops* first grew out of the jaw, they had a sharp point on top. But as the dinosaur used the teeth to eat, the point on each

Sauropods such as Diplodocus, *which lived about 150 million years ago, might have reared up on their hind limbs to feed on vegetation near the tops of tall trees. This idea was first proposed in the early 1900s, but not all paleontologists today agree that this was possible.*

tooth was worn down to form a flat surface. The points were probably worn down by grinding against plant material and other teeth.

Some dinosaurs that most paleontologists think ate plants do not have teeth with flat grinding surfaces on top. The teeth of *Iguanodon* and *Stegosaurus* look a little like Christmas trees from the side, but they are not as sharp or jagged as those of the meat eaters. One living animal that has similarly shaped teeth is the iguana, for which *Iguanodon* was named. Although most lizards are predatory meat or insect eaters, iguanas eat plants. This provides some evidence that *Iguanodon* and *Stegosaurus* might have been plant eaters, too.

The gigantic sauropods have neither sharply pointed cutting teeth nor flat-topped grinding teeth. Their teeth are either broad and spoon shaped, like those of *Camarasaurus*, or thin and pencil shaped, like those of *Diplodocus*. It's hard to envision the animal either eating meat or grinding up vegetation with teeth of these types.

How did they keep their enormous bodies fueled with food? One clue was found inside the rib cage of a well-preserved fossil sauropod skeleton. A set of rounded, polished stones, called gastroliths, was uncovered as the backbone and ribs were excavated. Most paleontologists have concluded that the sauropod had a gizzard, as most living birds and alligators do. Chickens, which have no teeth, swallow sand grains that collect in the gizzard, a muscular organ located between the mouth and the stomach. After the bird swallows the food, it passes through the gizzard, where it is ground up between the sand grains. Perhaps sauropods were similar. They may have used their teeth to cut twigs and shred leaves off branches. Then, after the plant material was swallowed, the stones in the gizzard may have ground it up before it passed into the stomach to be digested.

Once the plant-eating dinosaurs located their food, they wouldn't have had much problem "catching" it. Grasses, shrubs, and trees can't run away. But the story is different for meat eaters.

There are two mysteries about the feeding habits of meat-eating dinosaurs. First, were they active hunters that tracked down prey, attacked it, and killed it, or were they scavengers that fed off the carcasses of other dinosaurs? Secondly, did they hunt for food as individuals or in groups or packs? The fossils provide us with some evidence about these intriguing mysteries, but not enough to solve them for sure.

For example, most carnivorous dinosaurs, such as *Allosaurus* and *Deinonychus*, have arms and hands that appear to have been capable of grabbing other objects. Along with their sharp teeth with jagged edges, the long arms and hands would have been valuable to an active hunter in search of prey. Several skeletons of *Deinonychus* were found near a skeleton of a large contemporary plant eater, *Tenontosaurus*, in Wyoming. Many paleontologists believe that this grouping of skeletons implies that a pack of *Deinonychus* attacked and killed a solitary *Tenontosaurus* with their sickle-shaped claws and sharp teeth. This explanation is certainly possible. But it is also possible that several *Deinonychus*, attracted by the rotting carcass, came to scavenge on the body of the *Tenontosaurus* and ended up fighting over it.

In fact, some paleontologists believe that the "king" of dinosaurs was primarily a scavenger. *Tyrannosaurus* had very short arms ending in hands with only two fingers instead of the usual three; it could not even reach its mouth with its arms. For this reason, some paleontologists have suggested that, rather than an active hunter, *Tyrannosaurus* was a scavenger that looked for dead animals. But who knows? With its powerful legs and meat-cleaver jaws, it certainly had all the weapons it needed to be a most fearsome hunter.

In the late 1980s and early 1990s, some paleontologists argued that Tyrannosaurus was primarily a scavenger rather than an active hunter. Here two quarrel over a dead Alamosaurus.

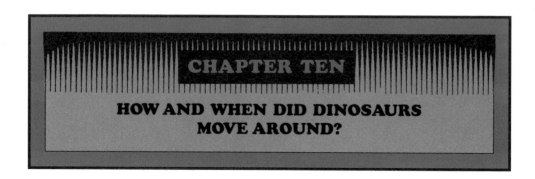

CHAPTER TEN

HOW AND WHEN DID DINOSAURS MOVE AROUND?

Fossil footprints of dinosaurs have been found in many places around the world. Along with fossil bones of dinosaurs, which have now been found on every modern continent, they have given us a lot of useful information about where dinosaurs lived and how they moved around.

We know, for example, that dinosaurs lived on land. Some walked and ran on their two back legs, while others got around on all four. We can generally make a pretty good guess about the way they moved, based on whether the front legs, or arms, are as long as the back legs. We can also look at modern relatives of extinct dinosaurs whose skeletons have a similar shape, and we can study the fossil trackways that some dinosaurs left behind, preserving a record of how their legs moved.

How they moved is easier to discover than *when*. For instance, we cannot tell whether dinosaurs moved around during the day or the night. Their fossils just don't give that kind of clue, and since all the large dinosaurs became extinct over 65 million years ago, we cannot go out and watch them. As with some living

Was Velociraptor a *hunter at night,* as shown in this sneak attack on a sleeping herd of Protoceratops? Perhaps, but fossils don't provide any good clues about which dinosaurs were active during the day and which roamed at night.

animal groups, like birds, perhaps some dinosaurs were active by day and others were "night owls."

Meat eaters, which generally had short front limbs compared to their hind limbs, usually moved around on their two back legs. We know that from examining their trackways. The trackways also show that the tail was usually held up in the air, because there is no impression left in the rock of the tail being dragged across the ground. In this way, the raised tail in back balanced the head and chest up front.

This picture differs somewhat from the one that scientists used to imagine, especially for large meat eaters such as *Allosaurus* and *Tyrannosaurus*. They were usually pictured as standing upright, with the tail dragging on the ground behind them. When standing still, they may well have stood more erect to scan the landscape for prey, but they probably ran and hunted with the body more horizontal.

The actual speed at which meat eaters ran is more difficult to be certain about. Much depends upon the mathematical formula that one uses to calculate the speed. It is usually based on the length of certain leg bones compared to the stride length pre-served in fossil trackways. For example, different scientists have estimated that the sprinting speed of *Tyrannosaurus* might have been as high as 45 miles (more than 70 kilometers) per hour or as low as 25 miles (40 kilometers) per hour. This range of speed is pretty fast for an animal thought to weigh between 4 and 8 tons. The fastest humans run about 22 miles (35 kilometers) per hour. Rhinoceroses, which weigh about 2 tons, can run about 28 miles (45 kilometers) per hour.

Giant sauropods, in contrast to meat eaters, usually walked on all four legs. Their front legs, or arms, and their back legs were about the same length. All were built very strong to support the animal's great weight. An adult *Apatosaurus* may have weighed between 30 and 40 tons. The largest land animal living today, the

African elephant, weighs only between 5 and 6 tons! The plant-eating sauropods probably were slower than the meat eaters. However, they may well have moved fairly fast when they needed to, like an elephant. Again, the actual speed at which these enormous dinosaurs moved is difficult to estimate, especially because there are so few fossil trackways known. The ones found so far suggest that sauropods moved at only about 2 miles (3 kilometers) per hour.

Do you remember how your body seems to weigh less when you get into a swimming pool or the ocean? Well, many scientists used to think that giant sauropods spent most of their time in the water to help support their great weight. They thought that the long neck might have been used as a snorkel so that most of the body could have been kept underwater, out of sight of predators.

But later, scientists realized that the weight of the water on a sauropod's chest would have been very great. Take a deep breath and notice how your chest gets bigger. Now press your hands against your ribs and notice how it's harder to take a breath. Your hands are like the weight of the water on a sauropod's chest. The weight of the water would have been too great to let a submerged sauropod breathe.

So now many scientists believe that, like the elephant, sauropods had strong legs that could support their great weight on land. The question is difficult to answer for sure because there are no close relatives of the sauropods living today. We can only make a guess by looking at a living mammal of similar shape.

Today scientists are arguing more about this question: Could sauropods, such as *Barosaurus*, occasionally rear up on their hind legs for feeding or defense? In 1991 the American Museum of Natural History constructed a new exhibit showing a mother *Barosaurus* rearing up on her hind legs to protect her baby from an attacking *Allosaurus*. The idea of sauropods rear-

ing up is not new. In the early 1900s, Charles R. Knight, the first famous dinosaur artist, painted a large sauropod rearing up on its hind legs to feed on young leaves near the top of a tree. Could these animals really do this?

In truth, we cannot be sure. Some scientists have argued that the bodies of some sauropods, such as that of *Barosaurus*, were built so that most of the dinosaur's weight was centered just in front of the hind legs, making it easier for the animal to rear up. Others have questioned whether the neck, shoulders, and hind legs were strong enough to allow the animal to raise its body this way. Still other paleontologists have wondered how the *Barosaurus*'s heart could have pumped enough blood up to the head to keep the animal from fainting, falling over, and injuring itself.

Such debates are common among people who study dinosaurs. Often there is just not enough information in the fossils to decide one way or the other. Indeed, the main reason the American Museum of Natural History built the *Barosaurus* mount was to draw attention to the fact that we cannot answer many interesting questions about the ways dinosaurs behaved.

A mother Barosaurus *rears up to defend her baby from an attacking* Allosaurus. *This scene may have occurred about 150 million years ago in what is now Utah or Wyoming.*

CHAPTER ELEVEN

WHAT COLOR WERE TYRANNOSAURUS, STEGOSAURUS, AND TRICERATOPS?

It's fun to imagine dinosaurs with spots or stripes or patches of yellow, pink, and blue. Why not? Think of the amazing colors of some birds and snakes, or the way some lizards can even change colors. True, no very large animals living today are quite that colorful, but perhaps dinosaurs were different. To be honest, we do not know.

The most common kinds of dinosaur fossils that we find are bones and teeth. These are the hardest and most durable parts of the animal. As a result, they do not disintegrate or decay as fast as softer organs, muscles, and skin, so they are the most likely parts of the body to last long enough to be buried by sediments and preserved as fossils.

Only rarely is dinosaur skin preserved in fossils. Even then, it's not the real skin. What we find is an imprint of the skin left in the mud that covered the carcass and eventually hardened into stone. The real skin rotted and disintegrated. All that remains is a mold of the skin's original texture, showing whether the skin was bumpy or smooth—in other words, what the skin would have felt like to touch.

However, no dinosaur fossil preserves the original color of the skin. Because no dinosaurs are around today, we can only guess what color they were by looking at the colors of modern animals.

Most early artists painted dinosaurs in dull greens and browns. At that time, dinosaurs were thought of as slow and stupid animals that lived in swampy jungles. More recently, our image of at least some dinosaurs has changed. Now they are popularly viewed as having been more intelligent and agile. Along with this new idea, a new idea about color has become popular. Now we often see more brightly colored illustrations of extinct dinosaurs. But in fact this is just a popular trend, and when you draw dinosaurs like *Tyrannosaurus* and *Stegosaurus*, you can make them any color you want.

A colorful male Triceratops *courts a less colorful female.*
In reality, we have no idea what colors Triceratops *was.*
Perhaps the female was more colorful than the male.
Fossils don't provide answers to these mysteries.

Early illustrations often showed Stegosaurus in dull greens or browns, like the one at the left, with its front legs sprawling out to the side and its tail dragging on the ground. The view at the right typifies the much more active and colorful interpretation of modern illustrations, with brighter colors, erect front legs, and a raised tail.

CHAPTER TWELVE

HOW WERE BABY DINOSAURS BORN?
DID DINOSAURS HAVE FAMILIES?

If we find enough bones and teeth to reconstruct a dinosaur skeleton, we can make some guesses about the animal's behavior, such as what it might have eaten, how it moved, and what kind of skeletal equipment it had to defend itself and attack others. But one question we haven't talked about yet is how baby dinosaurs were born. Fortunately, we have some very good clues to solve this mystery.

You wouldn't expect that anything as fragile as an egg could last long at all. We have to pack eggs in special containers just to get them home safely from the grocery store. So to think of them lasting millions of years seems quite unrealistic. Nevertheless, we know for sure that dinosaurs laid eggs because their fossilized eggs have been found. The most famous dinosaur eggs were discovered back in 1923, during an expedition to Mongolia organized by the American Museum of Natural History. The expedition's fossil collectors found nests of eggs that probably belonged to the dinosaur *Protoceratops*, an early relative of *Triceratops*. They also found numerous skulls of *Protoceratops* that document how newly hatched babies grew up to become adults.

The discovery of dinosaur eggs and nests created a worldwide public sensation. Newspapers and magazines published dozens of articles about the eggs and nests. However, apart from the surprise that these eggs could be preserved for so long as fossils, the discovery of dinosaur eggs really should not have surprised us too much. Dinosaurs are sauropsids, or reptiles, and all reptiles lay eggs, including turtles, lizards, snakes, and crocodiles. So dinosaurs should be expected to reproduce just like all their reptilian cousins.

During the 1980s, many other dinosaur nests with eggs were discovered in the United States and Canada—a few even with skeletons of unborn babies inside the eggs! These discoveries have led many paleontologists to suggest that dinosaur parents took care of their babies for some time after they were born. Again, we cannot be sure if they did, because all the large dinosaurs are extinct, so we cannot go out and watch to see if they took care of their young. However, it should not surprise us if they did to some degree, because the closest living relatives of these dinosaurs—birds and crocodiles—care for their developing young in the nest.

Because many dinosaur nests are sometimes found in the same small area, some paleontologists believe that at least some dinosaurs might have nested and moved around in herds. It has even been suggested that some dinosaurs might have migrated over long distances each year. Occasionally, paleontologists find fossil trackways that show many individual dinosaurs of the same kind moving in the same direction. However, it is often hard to be sure that they were all moving at the same time in a group. Sometimes paleontologists also find huge collections of fossil bones of one kind of dinosaur, suggesting that a whole herd was killed at the same time by a disastrous flood, volcanic eruption, or other natural calamity. On the other hand, the flow of river currents can create large collections of bones without the dinosaurs necessarily having been grouped into herds when they were alive.

In all, it's difficult to be certain whether extinct dinosaurs migrated or traveled in herds. But since birds—extinct dinosaurs' closest living relatives—often travel in flocks, it's not unreasonable to assume that some kinds of extinct dinosaurs might also have lived and traveled in social groups.

Crocodiles and birds, the closest living relatives of extinct dinosaurs, both lay eggs and take care of the nest as their young are developing inside the egg and hatching. So, we should not be too surprised to find nests and eggs of extinct dinosaurs. They may well have cared for their young, but we cannot tell exactly how much care they provided.

CHAPTER THIRTEEN

WHAT KILLED ALL
THE LARGE DINOSAURS?

Because we can tell how long ago dinosaurs lived by dating some of the layers of rock in which they were fossilized, we know that all of the large dinosaurs, such as *Tyrannosaurus*, *Triceratops*, *Anatotitan*, *Ankylosaurus*, and *Pachycephalosaurus*, became extinct about 65 million years ago. And dinosaurs were by no means the only group affected. In the oceans, microscopic organisms, clams, snails, mosasaurs, ichthyosaurs, plesiosaurs, and ammonites, shelled animals related to the living nautilus, were either totally or partially killed off. On land, many kinds of mammals became extinct. What caused so many species to die out?

The mystery surrounding the extinction of most dinosaurs has long been one of the most fascinating questions in all of science. As a result, scientists have come up with many different explanations about what caused the extinctions. Most ideas have been hard either to prove or disprove with the information we have to work with. For example, some paleontologists have suggested that dinosaurs died out because of a severe worldwide disease, or epidemic. As we have discussed in earlier chapters, most dinosaur fossils are bones or teeth, and many diseases would not have affected bones or teeth. So most fossils cannot tell us much about whether dinosaurs suffered from illnesses affecting the heart, lungs, stomach, kidneys, or bloodstream. However, most diseases tend to make only one or two kinds of animals sick—for example, only horses or only cows or only humans. So it's a little hard to imagine one particular disease killing off all the different kinds of dinosaurs that were alive about 65 million years ago, not to mention all the other kinds of plants and animals that were affected.

Most scientists today believe that the widespread extinction of dinosaurs and other animals resulted from severe changes in the Earth's environment or climate. However, these same scientists differ on what caused the environmental changes.

One old idea is that, just before the end of the Age of Dinosaurs, many shallow seas had flooded large areas of many of the Earth's continents. For example, earlier chapters have mentioned the sea extending through North America from the Gulf of Mexico all the way up to the Arctic Ocean. Many kinds of dinosaurs lived along the coastal plains of this sea. The sea helped keep air temperature fairly warm and stable. The days, even in summer, were not too hot, and the nights, even in winter, were not too cold. At the end of the Age of Dinosaurs, for some reason that we are not sure about, this sea dried up. As a result, the summers got hotter and the winters got colder. Scientists long thought that dinosaurs could not survive these hot summers and cold winters, and so they perished. However, shallow seas like this one had flooded onto the continents and dried up at many other times during the Age of Dinosaurs. So, why would this event have caused so much extinction?

Because many scientists were not satisfied with the theory involving the shallow seas, some came up with new explanations about how the dinosaurs became extinct. The two explanations now most commonly discussed involve either a large volcanic event or the idea that one or more comets or asteroids hit the Earth. There is some evidence to support both these ideas.

At the end of the Age of Dinosaurs, the Earth had many volcanoes that threw out huge amounts of volcanic rock. The largest amount erupted out of cracks in the surface of the Earth in what is now India. These and other major eruptions could have released great quantities of volcanic gases and other small particles into the air. Over both short and long periods, the gases and particles circulating in the atmosphere could have dramatically changed the climate and increased air pollution on the Earth. Such pollution could have killed the plants and animals that dinosaurs fed on, and thus eventually might have killed the dinosaurs about 65 million years ago.

Competing with the volcanic explanation is the theory that one or more comets hit the Earth at that time. In thin layers of rock that mark the end of the Age of Dinosaurs, scientists have discovered high levels of some elements, such as iridium, that are found in comets but rare in the Earth's crust, or outer layer. They have also found microscopic crystals of a common mineral called quartz. These crystals were fractured by some event that released a tremendous amount of energy, like the impact of a comet on the Earth. Scientists who favor this idea suggest that the explosion

A group of Anatotitan, *members of the duckbill family, watch as an asteroid or comet streaks across the sky just before colliding with the Earth. Many scientists today believe that such an event, along with the resulting dust cloud and other effects, caused the extinction of large dinosaurs about 65 million years ago. Other scientists argue that widespread volcanic activity was responsible.*

resulting from the impact sent a huge cloud of dust into the Earth's atmosphere that blocked out most sunlight for several months or a year. As a result, plants, which need sunlight to grow, were killed. In turn, the animals that ate plants died, and finally, the meat eaters that ate plant eaters also died.

Both explanations are possible, and scientists are still debating about which is more likely to have caused the extinction of so many dinosaurs. However, it is difficult to be sure about what caused these extinctions so long ago because no humans were around to observe the events and because different scientific clues to the mystery suggest different explanations.

In 1992 scientists reported some important new evidence suggesting that an impact did indeed occur at the end of the Age of Dinosaurs. A crater in the Earth in the Yucatán Peninsula of Mexico was found to have been made, as nearly as we can tell, at the same time as the extinction of most dinosaurs.

However, we still have some problems to solve involving these extinctions. One problem is that we can't "tell time" in the ancient past well enough to be sure about how quickly or slowly the extinction of dinosaurs occurred. Did it happen in less than one year, as would be required if only a single impact occurred, or did it take tens or hundreds of thousands of years, as multiple volcanic eruptions or multiple impacts would require? Our ability to date the layers of rock containing the dinosaurs and the iridium is just not good enough to tell for sure. Also, we don't yet understand very well why some of the Earth's plants and animals survived the disaster and others did not.

All in all it is not surprising that scientists are not sure what killed most dinosaurs about 65 million ago because 65 million years is a long, long time. Just remember, President John F. Kennedy was killed only about thirty years ago, and dozens of people actually witnessed the assassination. Yet experts still don't agree about who caused his death.

CHAPTER FOURTEEN

ARE ALL THE DINOSAURS EXTINCT?

If you try to follow your family history back in time, you begin with your two parents. Before them came their parents, your grandparents. And before your grandparents came your great-grandparents. Your parents, grandparents, and great-grandparents are your ancestors, and they, along with your other relatives, including brothers, sisters, cousins, aunts, and uncles, all make up your family.

That idea extends to ancestors and relatives in evolution, but the further back we go, the more difficult it becomes to identify ancestors. We may not know exactly what the ancestor looked like, but we do know which groups were closely related. By looking at the members of the family, we can see that they all share some features that originated in and were inherited from that ancestor.

In the same way that you came from your great-grandparents, all the different kinds of dinosaurs came from the first dinosaur. Birds came from a dinosaur, too! Since the early 1980s, a huge amount of evidence has been put together to show that birds are members of the dinosaur family.

Let's look at some of the physical features of dinosaurs that birds inherited. In chapter 5, we discovered that a dinosaur is a reptile, or sauropsid, with legs that go straight down from its hips to the ground. Look at a chicken or pigeon or ostrich and you'll notice that the legs go straight down to the ground, just like the legs of dinosaurs.

Within the whole family of dinosaurs, birds are closest cousins to the meat-eating dinosaurs, such as *Allosaurus* and especially *Deinonychus*. The feet of a chicken, a pigeon, and an ostrich all have three fully developed toes that point forward, with the middle toe the longest. This is the same type of foot structure we find in *Allosaurus*, *Deinonychus*, and *Compsognathus*. We can conclude, then, that birds inherited their foot structure from some meat-eating dinosaur. In fact,

Fossils of Velociraptor *have been found in Mongolia, where it lived during the last part of the Age of Dinosaurs. It is shown reaching out to grasp a juvenile* Protoceratops. *The structure of its hind legs and arms has now convinced most paleontologists that* Velociraptor *was a close relative of the earliest birds, such as* Archaeopteryx.

the skeleton of the earliest known bird, *Archaeopteryx*, which lived about 140 million years ago, is so similar in its structure and size to the skeleton of *Compsognathus* that one specimen of *Archaeopteryx* was misidentified for decades before anyone realized it. The main difference between *Archaeopteryx* and *Compsognathus* is that we know *Archaeopteryx* had feathers, like modern birds, and there is no evidence that *Compsognathus* or *Deinonychus* had feathers.

Because birds and small meat-eating dinosaurs have so many of the same bony features in their skeletons, most scientists now think that a small meat-eating dinosaur was the ancestor of all birds. They argue that birds are not a separate family from dinosaurs. In an evolutionary sense, they *are* dinosaurs—feathered dinosaurs!

Most paleontologists consider *Archaeopteryx* the oldest-known fossil bird. It shares many skeletal features with other small theropods that also lived about 150 million years ago. This evidence has led many to conclude that birds are evolutionary descendants of dinosaurs and belong to the dinosaur family.

Now if birds are really dinosaurs with feathers, then we can solve part of another mystery: Were dinosaurs warm-blooded? In other words, could dinosaurs keep a steady body temperature, as we do, without moving into the sunlight to warm up or moving into the shade to cool off?

Over the last couple of decades, some paleontologists have presented evidence suggesting that many extinct dinosaurs may have been warm-blooded. For example, the erect posture of dinosaurs, in which the legs go straight down to the ground from the hips, is similar to the posture found in active, warm-blooded mammals, including humans. Also, microscopic examination of the bone structure found in some extinct dinosaurs implies that they grew up rapidly and were capable of periods of high activity. Unfortunately, however, this evidence cannot be used to tell whether extinct dinosaurs were always very active or just occasionally so. Thus, we cannot be sure about the extent to which extinct dinosaurs were warm-blooded.

Nonetheless, if birds *are* feathered dinosaurs, then we know that at least some dinosaurs are warm-blooded. We can be sure that birds are warm-blooded because we can measure their body temperature and observe that they keep it at a fairly constant level.

It may well be that small meat eaters, such as *Compsognathus* and *Deinonychus*, were also warm-blooded because they are such close cousins to living birds. However, because they are extinct, we cannot be as sure about this feature as we can about foot shape, for example. It's even more difficult to say whether the large dinosaurs such as *Tyrannosaurus*, *Barosaurus*, *Triceratops*, and *Stegosaurus* were warm-blooded because none of them are still living, and they have no close living relatives.

Although *Tyrannosaurus*, *Stegosaurus*, and other large dinosaurs are extinct, it's clear that some dinosaurs are still living. In fact, one may be perched in a tree outside your window! So, what color is that dinosaur?

71

GLOSSARY

ammonite (AM-on-ite)—a group of extinct sea-dwelling mollusks, related to today's squid, octopus, and nautilus. Ammonites lived from about 400 million to 65 million years ago.

amnion (AM-nee-on)—a watertight membrane inside an egg that forms a fluid-filled sack to keep the developing embryo from drying out and dying.

amniotes (AM-nee-oats)—animals with an amnion inside their egg, such as mammals and birds, dinosaurs, and other reptiles.

ankylosaurs (an-KI-lo-sawrs)—an extinct group of ornithischian dinosaurs that had bony armor over most of the body.

blue-green algae—a group of primarily microscopic, single-celled life-forms that have no nucleus in the cell but can make food for themselves by using sunlight. Among the earliest-known forms of life.

carnivorous—eating food that consists entirely of animal parts.

ceratopsians (cer-a-TOP-see-ans)—an extinct group of or-nithischian dinosaurs that usually had horns and a collar of bone on the skull.

cold-blooded—not maintaining a constant internal body tem-perature, either heating up or cooling down as a result of the temperature outside the body.

evolution—the process through which life-forms change from generation to generation as descendants inherit modified physical features from their ancestors.

extinct—no members of the group still living.

fossil—any trace of ancient life, such as bones, teeth, shells, and footprints, that has been largely replaced by minerals over time but retains its basic original shape.

fossilization—the natural process by which a fossil is formed.

gastroliths (GAS-tro-liths)—rounded stones found in the rib cage of a few fossil dinosaur skeletons. The stones are thought to have been swallowed to help grind up food inside the ani-mal's gizzard.

hadrosaurs (HAD-ro-sawrs)—an extinct group of ornithischian di-nosaurs with a bony, ducklike "bill" at the front of the skull.

herbivorous—eating food that consists entirely of plants.

ichthyosaurs (IK-thee-o-sawrs)—an extinct group of porpoiselike reptiles that lived in the oceans from about 250 million to 65 million years ago.

iridium (ear-ID-ee-um)—a heavy metallic element common in asteroids and comets but rare in the outer crust of the Earth.

mammals—a group of animals with backbones, including hu-mans, that have hair and nurse their newborn with milk.

mosasaurs (MO-za-sawrs)—an extinct group of large lizards that lived in the oceans from about 100 million to 65 million years ago.

nautilus (NAW-til-us)—a sea-dwelling mollusk with a spiral shell that is distantly related to the squid and octopus; early close relatives of the nautilus appeared over 500 million years ago.

ornithischians (or-ni-THISH-ee-ans)—an extinct group of dinosaurs, including ankylosaurs, stegosaurs, hadrosaurs, ceratopsians, and pachycephalosaurs. These dinosaurs all have pubic bones that point toward the back end of the animal.

pachycephalosaurs (pack-ee-CEF-al-o-sawrs)—an extinct group of ornithischian dinosaurs with a thick bony cap on top of the skull.

paleontologists (pay-lee-on-TOL-o-gists)—scientists who study ancient life by collecting and analyzing fossils.

plesiosaurs (PLEAS-ee-o-sawrs)—an extinct group of long-necked reptiles with front and hind flippers that lived in the oceans from about 220 million to 65 million years ago.

predators—animals that get their food by hunting and eating other animals.

pterosaurs (TER-o-sawrs)—an extinct group of flying reptiles. They lived from about 200 million to 65 million years ago.

quartz—a mineral that is common in the Earth's crust.

saurischians (sawr-ISH-ee-ans)—a group of dinosaurs with offset thumbs for grasping.

sauropods (SAWR-o-pods)—an extinct group of giant saurischian dinosaurs with extremely long necks.

sauropsids (sawr-OP-sids)—a group of animals with backbones and a special opening in the roof of the mouth. They include extinct dinosaurs as well as modern birds, lizards, snakes, and other reptiles.

stegosaurs (STEG-o-sawrs)—an extinct group of ornithischian dinosaurs with distinctive arrangements of bony plates and spikes along the neck, back, and tail.

synapsids (sin-AP-sids)—a group of animals with backbones, including mammals and their extinct relatives, whose skulls have an opening behind each eye socket.

tetrapods (TET-ra-pods)—a group of animals with backbones, including amphibians, reptiles, mammals, and their extinct relatives, that also have four limbs with distinct ankles, wrists, toes, and fingers.

theropods (THER-o-pods)—a group of saurischian dinosaurs that have three forward-pointing toes on the hind feet, with the middle toe being the longest.

trackway—a sequence of fossil footprints left by an ancient animal.

vertebrates (VER-te-brates)—a group of animals with a backbone composed of many individual bones called vertebrae.

warm-blooded—maintaining a fairly constant internal body temperature that is not affected much by the temperature outside the body.

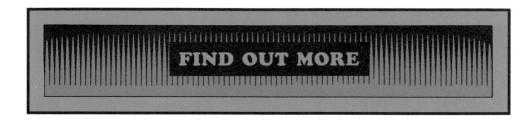

FIND OUT MORE

Of the dozens of books about dinosaurs that are available, these are especially helpful.

British Museum of Natural History. *Dinosaurs and Their Living Relatives*. 2nd ed. New York: Cambridge University Press, 1986.

Gaffney, E.S. *A Golden Guide of Dinosaurs*. New York: Golden Press, 1990.

Norell, Mark. *All You Need to Know About Dinosaurs*. New York: Sterling Publishing Co., 1991.

Norman, David. *Illustrated Encyclopedia of Dinosaurs*. New York: Outlet Book Co., 1985.

_____. *When Dinosaurs Ruled the Earth*. New York: Simon & Schuster, 1985.

Wallace, J. *Familiar Dinosaurs*. New York: Chanticleer Press, 1993.

INDEX

79

ABOUT THE AUTHOR AND ARTIST

A paleontologist with a lifelong fascination with dinosaurs, Lowell Dingus is currently associated with the American Museum of Natural History in New York City. There, as exhibition coordinator and project director for permanent and temporary exhibits on vertebrate paleontology, he has been responsible for developing displays that bring prehistoric times to life for museum goers. He previously served as scientific coordinator for exhibits on evolutionary history at the California Academy of Sciences in San Francisco, a post he took after completing a doctorate in paleontology and postdoctoral research in geology at the University of California at Berkeley. Dr. Dingus has done fieldwork in Montana, Oregon, California, and Mongolia and has written for scientific journals and popular magazines. This is his first book for children.

Stephen C. Quinn is an artist and exhibit designer for the American Museum of Natural History where he's worked for the past twenty years. In addition to illustrating prehistoric subjects for the museum, he's led natural history trips to Antarctica, Africa, South America, and Europe. A member of the Society of Animal Artists, Mr. Quinn has done illustrations for Harper & Row's *Field Guide to North American Wildlife*, as well as for *The New York Times Magazine* and The New York Zoological Society. Books on dinosaurs were Mr. Quinn's favorites when he was a boy.